LIVING FRACTALS

Midge Turing

Edited by
Stephen Barnwell

Antarctica Arts
MMXXIII

Other Books from Antarctica Arts

Lost Journals of Phineas Finke
Ikonographica
Willoughby's World Of Wonder
Oneirognosis, the Art of Dreaming
Far Country
MoneyArt
Capital Offenses
Equinox, A Coloring Book
Angelikon, A Coloring Book
DreamTime, A Coloring Book

The illustrations in this book were created with the assistance of an Artificial Intelligence.

Published by Antarctica Arts

www.AntarcticaArts.com

ISBN 978-1-7339649-7-5

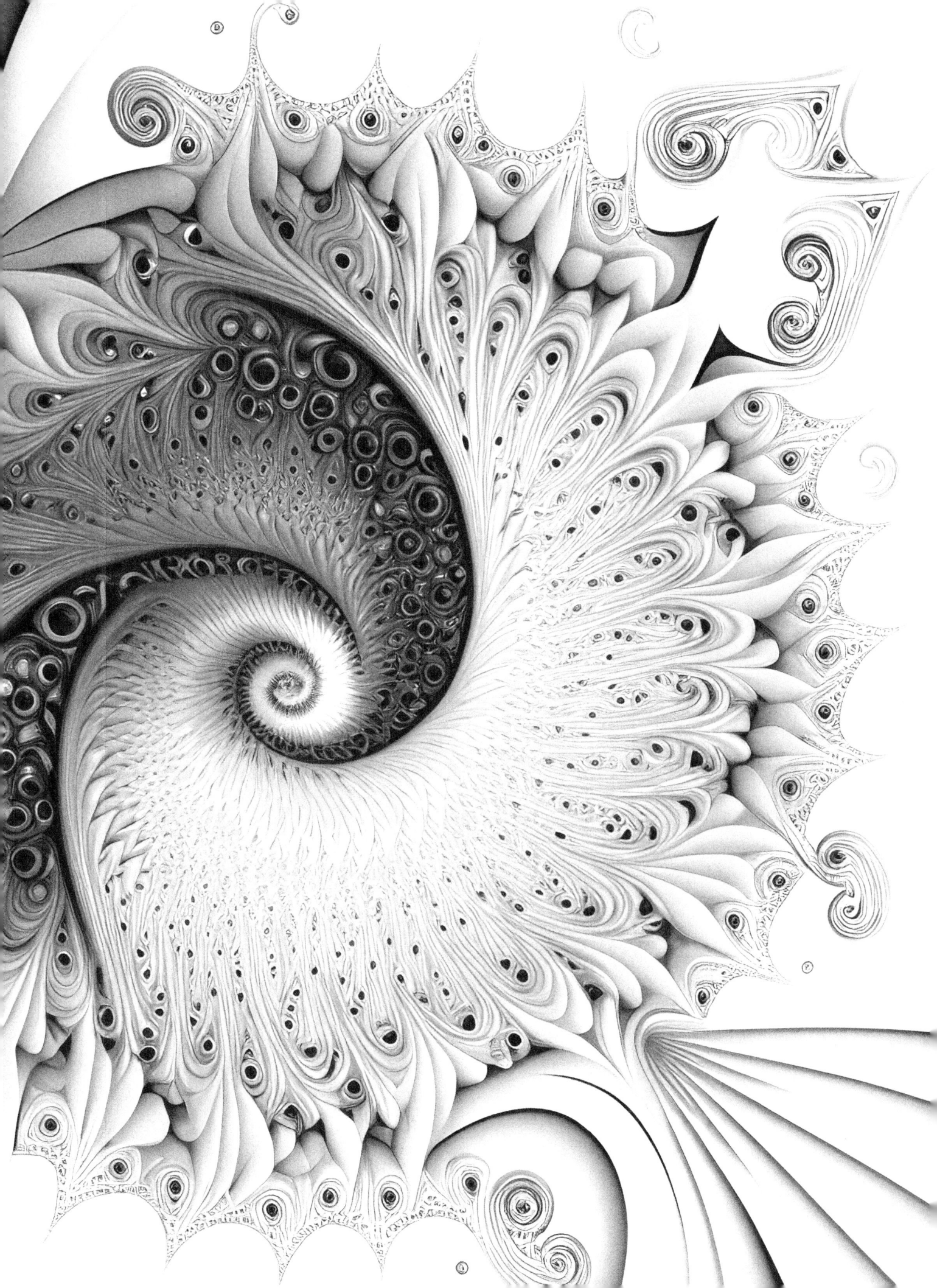

Printed in Great Britain
by Amazon